PUPPIES
KW-023

Contents

Overleaf: Like all other puppies, these Cocker Spaniel youngsters enjoy socialization with their littermates. **Title page:** When choosing a puppy, look for one that is friendly and happy. He is the one for you.

Photography: Dr. Herbert R. Axelrod, Tom Caravaglia, Isabelle Francais, Sal Micelli, Ron Reagan, Vincent Serbin, Sally Anne Thompson, Louise Van Der Meid, Ake Wintzell.

The portrayal of canine pet products in this book is for general instructive value only; the appearance of such products does not necessarily constitute an endorsement by the author, the publisher, or the owners of the dogs portrayed in this book.

© Copyright 1989 by TFH Publications Inc.

Distributed in the UNITED STATES by T.F.H. Publications, Inc., One T.F.H. Plaza, Neptune City, NJ 07753; in CANADA to the Pet Trade by H & L Pet Supplies Inc., 27 Kingston Crescent, Kitchener, Ontario N2B 2T6; Rolf C. Hagen Ltd., 3225 Sartelon Street, Montreal 382 Quebec; in CANADA to the Book Trade by Macmillan of Canada (A Division of Canada Publishing Corporation), 164 Commander Boulevard, Agincourt, Ontario M1S 3C7; in ENGLAND by T.F.H. Publications Limited, Cliveden House/Priors Way/Bray, Maidenhead, Berkshire SL6 2HP, England; in AUSTRALIA AND THE SOUTH PACIFIC by T.F.H. (Australia) Pty. Ltd., Box 149, Brookvale 2100 N.S.W., Australia; in NEW ZEALAND by Ross Haines & Son, Ltd., 18 Monmouth Street, Grey Lynn, Auckland 2, New Zealand; in SINGAPORE AND MALAYSIA by MPH Distributors (S) Pte., Ltd., 601 Sims Drive, #03/07/21, Singapore 1438; in the PHILIPPINES by Bio-Research, 5 Lippay Street, San Lorenzo Village, Makati Rizal; in SOUTH AFRICA by Multipet Pty. Ltd., 30 Turners Avenue, Durban 4001. Published by T.F.H. Publications, Inc. Manufactured in the United States of America by T.F.H. Publications, Inc.

PUPPIES

GABRIELLE FORBUSH

The tiny Yorkshire Terrier is a good choice of pet for an apartment dweller. **Below:** *This mixed breed pup is well acclimated to the presence of his feline housemate.*

Selecting
Your New
Puppy

The decision to purchase a dog for a pet is an important one, and it should not be taken lightly. Once taken into a home, a dog becomes a true member of the family—a loyal, loving companion who will do his best to serve and protect his master. The ownership of a dog carries a good deal of responsibility, for a dog is a living thing that requires supervision, food, shelter, exercise, periodic medical attention, love and affection. Buying the dog itself is the primary purchase, but leashes, collars, food, licenses and inoculations are all a part of the entire outlay that will be necessary. Thus, it is plain to see that buying a dog is a

responsibility that should be thoughtfully undertaken.

Once your family has decided that a dog would be a welcome addition to the household—and the *entire* family must be in accord—there are a number of other decisions that need to be made. Your primary decision will concern the selection of a particular breed and its suitability to your lifestyle.

It is obvious that you should not get a Great Dane for an efficiency apartment, but on the other hand, the massive Bulldog is a surprisingly good dog for a small home because of his calm temperament and need for little exercise. As you can see, size can be deceiving, and if you have a particular liking for a certain size or breed of dog it is best to first read up on the living requirements of that breed before choosing or deciding against it. Generally speaking, if you are an apartment dweller, you would do best by selecting a member of the Toy Group. If you are away for most of the day, a sedate—rather than highly energetic—dog would be the logical choice.

Other decisions you must make as a prospective pet owner include whether to buy a male or female dog and whether you want to pay the price of a purebred puppy. Depending on how involved you care to get in the dog fancy, you may or may not want to buy a show dog that has a pedigree (a certificate attesting to a dog's breeding lineage) and is registered with the national dog breed registry. Showing dogs is quite a separate sport, one that could be written about in another volume!

WHERE TO BUY

You can choose among several places to buy your dog. Many people think of their local pet shop as the first source for buying a puppy, and very often they're right; you should remember, however, that a pet shop cannot possibly stock all breeds of dog. If your pet shop does not carry the type of dog you desire, there are other places to look. One is a kennel whose business is breeding show-quality dogs; such kennels may have extra pups for sale. Another source is the one-dog owner who wants to sell the puppies from an occasional litter to pay the expenses of his small-scale breeding operation. To find such kennels and part-time breeders and hobbyists, check the classified section of your local newspaper or look in your telephone directory.

At the other end of the spectrum are those lovable mixed breeds. These dogs, like the purebreds, come in a variety of shapes, sizes and colors, but their parentage is generally not the result of a deliberate, well-planned (genetically speaking) mating. Still, mongrels can provide as

As puppies, Golden Retrievers are adorable little charmers; as adult dogs, they are handsome, loyal companions.

much love and devotion as any purebred, and such a dog would be a good choice for the family on a limited budget, provided the family has chosen its dog with special care. The animal shelters are full of unwanted dogs who would surely love to be taken into a kind home. If you can open your home to such an animal, you would be doing a good deed for the animal and yourself.

CHECKING YOUR PUP'S HEALTH

Once you have decided on a Boston Terrier, a Scottie, a German Shepherd Dog, a mixed

A Papillon puppy flanked by two kitten friends. If your household is to be shared by a pup and a kitten, allow the two to get acquainted early, so there will be no rivalry as they grow. **Above:** The Yorkshire Terrier, with its lively personality, is sure to perk up anyone's home.

breed—whatever, you can begin the actual search for that one special puppy that is to share your life for years to come. The first prerequisite is to look for good health and physical appearance. A puppy can hardly have one without the other. Choose only a healthy dog. If you get a weakling at a bargain price, be sure it is really a bargain. Veterinarian's bills or the loss of the little thing after nursing it along may more than balance a few dollars saved.

If a puppy has dull or red eyes, is listless, won't come even when you coax (let alone tumble out of the box, his tail wagging frantically), if his coat is rough or has bare spots, if his legs are bandy or too thin—beware. Go

The sex of a puppy, and whether or not it will be altered, are but two of the factors to consider before you choose a pup.

over even the peppy, playful, roly-poly pup carefully. Look inside of and smell his ears. If there is a brown matter and bad odor, he has ear canker or mites. Have this cleared up before you take him home.

His teeth should be white, his gums pink and not grayish or inflamed red. See that there is no inflammation around the tail, on the paws or stomach. Feel his bone structure by running your hand over his legs and down his back; get the texture of his coat. He should have a clean "puppy smell" all over, in breath and body. Be wary if he resents your examining him, as he should think of this as a game and should be wiggling and licking you, wanting to play.

In handling a puppy, never pull him up by his front legs or with your hands behind his shoulders, as this may seriously injure him. Pick him up "fore and aft," one hand under his chest and the other raising the hindquarters. Hold him with his hind legs resting on your arm against your body; in this position he'll feel secure and protected. Teach all children who may play with the young puppy how to properly pick him up. Children who are seen yanking the puppy's leg or tail are too young to responsibly handle such a frail living thing and should be allowed to see the dog only under strict adult supervision. You might tell them that if they hurt him, he

has the right to protect himself in the only way he knows! Rough treatment as a puppy can lead to a poorly adjusted adult.

And so—your puppy is yours! From now on, you and he are "for keeps." It will be a big comfort to you to have a veterinarian thoroughly check him out before he is permanently placed in your home. Your vet also will administer the necessary inoculations to guard your dog against the diseases that might otherwise plague him, that is if inoculations have not already been taken care of by the breeder. It is indeed a good idea to get your new pup accustomed to his vet as soon as possible so that when he goes to the vet's for periodic check-ups or for treatment, he will not be frightened by the surroundings.

Buying from a recognized source is helpful for an inexperienced dog owner, as you have someone to consult when problems arise. However, don't run to him for every little thing. Be prepared to take care of your own dog and to take such good care in the matters of cleanliness, food, and exercise that he doesn't reach the stage where expert treatment is needed. However, if you ever feel he does need it, give your dog and your veterinarian a break. Bring them together at the first hint of any serious trouble—this is the only way to prevent problems from developing further.

The Keeshond, a hardy breed, will need much outdoor activity. **Above:** The West Highland White Terrier, or "Westie," a small active breed, can make a good apartment pet. **Facing page:** A Cairn Terrier and a Westie. Both breeds are known for their spunk and vigor.

SHOULD YOU CHOOSE A FEMALE?

Many people believe that a female dog, commonly known as a bitch, will be a friendlier pet and one more loyal to her home and family. Although a female is less likely to become a neighborhood rover, the unspayed female will come into season twice a year and therefore attract eager males from far and wide. This, no doubt, would be somewhat of an annoyance to you and the neighborhood. If you purchase a female puppy, you will be faced with an important decision.

Should you have your female spayed? (Please do not say "spaded" as thousands of ill-informed people do.) The answer is "yes," although there are several arguments against spaying. Let us discuss them first. It is said that the spayed female will become lazy and fat. It is also said that spaying will make her subject to urinary, that is kidney, trouble later on, and that she will be unable to control her urinary flow as she gets older.

Neither argument is particularly valid. Dogs, spayed or not, often do get too fat. If they get fat they get lazy, and fat dogs, more often than thin ones, suffer from kidney trouble as they get older. A fat dog is fattened by his owner!

The spaying operation removes the ovaries. This interrupts and stops the estrus cycle, so that the female will not only *not* conceive, but she will have no estrus flow and she will not attract males. If the operation is performed on a very young puppy, the normal growth of the dog, physically and mentally, can be affected. There is no doubt that the growth and development of the ovaries play an important part in the growth of the animal. A puppy spayed when very young will, in some respects, always remain a puppy. She will have no sexual interests and none of the drives associated with sex, which the normal female would have. Lacking these interests, she might become lazy, spoil easily, and tend to become overweight.

A female dog will have her first season sometime around six months and before she is a year old. If she is a normal dog, it will then be another six months before she has her second. She will, therefore, be a mature dog mentally and physically before the second heat.

That first heat period suddenly awakens all the matronly instincts in the young female. She looks at other dogs with a greater and different interest—a mature interest. She also changes somewhat in her attitudes toward her master and her home. She will never lose those interests, nor that maturity of outlook.

Therefore, if she is spayed shortly after her first heat period, the operation will not affect her seriously, either physically or mentally. She will always maintain

Puppies are curious little characters, and this perky Yorkshire Terrier pup is no exception!

Above: These Westie puppies are characteristically alert and curious. The pup you choose should have these qualities. *Facing page:* This Irish Setter and his companion, a Miniature Poodle, have been friends since puppyhood. Pups that are raised together can become inseparable buddies.

a mature interest in everything, although she will never accept a male nor attract one.

She will not get fat, unless you overfeed or fail to exercise her. Neither will she be any more prone to kidney trouble than other dogs, spayed or not, females or males.

There is another reason for spaying. There is good evidence that the female sex hormones tend, in some cases, to stimulate uterine and breast cancer in older dogs. A prominent veterinary college now advises spaying all older females no longer intended for matronly duties as a means of preventing these cancers, thus prolonging their lives.

This writer has had considerable experience hunting with spayed females. In all cases, the females were mature animals before being spayed. One had had several litters of puppies. Kidney trouble did not develop in any of the dogs, and they hunted until they were ten years or older with no loss of hunting instinct.

WHAT ABOUT A MALE?

This section deals with females, and yet the inevitable question comes up: What about the males? The equivalent operation in the male is called castration. Should it be performed? Will it keep your dog from becoming a rover? Will it affect him physically?

Castration does cause serious bodily changes in the male.

Unless it is performed when he is very young, it will not keep him at home. It will not prevent him from biting if he's going to be a biter.

Thus, if a dog has been castrated after he has had sexual experiences with a female, his sexual urges will remain the same. He will chase the females just as intently as the intact males, and he will mate with them when he can. The only difference will be that the female cannot conceive from the mating.

To return to your female, you will want her to be a mature dog mentally and to have all the interests in life that a mature dog should have. Spay her after she has had a complete estrual season, and her outlook will always remain that of the intact female.

Now, how will you care for your female during her first heat period? Let's assume you live in a city, on a crowded street. You may have a fenced yard, but the males will come from miles around, and they'll congregate in the neighbors' yards, get into fights there, dirty in them, etc. They may come onto the porch to anoint the screens and to relieve themselves.

There are numerous lotions and liquids on the market that are supposed to keep the males away. Such preparations do not, however, change the natural urges of the female. When she is ready to accept a male, she'll go

Most people find it hard to resist a puppy's sweet, soulful expression, such as this Boxer pup exhibits.

hunting for one. She'll court him, and he will overcome any distaste he may have at first for the anti-mating odor on her. Confinement is the best precaution.

Still, you are not helpless in this situation. Select a vacant lot some distance from your house. Take your dog to this lot to relieve herself; if you can, take her by car. If you can't, pet stores sell canine sanitary napkins or you can make

one simply enough. At all other times keep your dog indoors, either in the basement or in an upstairs room to avoid having her possibly bolt out.

When a female is in season, she instinctively tries to attract a male to her. She does this by urinating in as many places as possible. Involuntary blood and estrual droppings help, too. The wind is certain to carry these

Different breeds have different requirements for overall maintenance, so be sure to read up on many breeds before you decide on a particular pup.

odors to some male, and shortly he arrives. That's why it's important to take the female to the vacant lot by car, or while she is wearing a sanitary napkin. If you walk her there, she'll piddle a bit on the way, or estrual droppings will leave a trail for the male.

If you follow the outlined system, however, you'll have little trouble—but only if you can keep a diligent watch on her.

THE NEW FAMILY MEMBER

You've "played fair," picking a pup you think will fit well into your family. Now play fair by seeing that he has a chance to do so.

You like a room to yourself and probably have your own favorite chair. He has a right to his own corner or bed, too. A dog does a good deal of meditating during a day, and plenty of sleeping, too. Even the wildest, most rollicking

King Charles Spaniels, with their outgoing, friendly character, can get along well with other dogs.

Beagle puppies settling down for nap time. Always respect your pup's wishes when it wants to rest or sleep.

pup needs time for both. Respect his rights and make others, children especially, leave him alone at such times.

A dog's bed is his castle. His must be warm, dry, and out of drafts. Since your dog may grow quickly, his first bed can start as a large carton or box, lined with newspapers and possibly a soft baby blanket. He may feel lonely and cry for a night or two. Place his bed by yours, so that you can reach down, pat him during the night, and soothe him with your voice. He will soon feel at home, day or night, and you can then move his bed to some other spot.

If his bed is to be in the corner of the kitchen or in a dry basement, be sure he is out of drafts. His permanent box, as he grows larger, may be lined with cedar shavings, straw or papers, aired or changed frequently. A commercially made dog bed that can be purchased at your local pet shop will supply him with all the comforts and warmth he could need. If he sleeps outdoors, provide a roofed box or dog house with a raised floor and an entrance that is not open to the wind. A burlap bag, which hangs in the doorway and which he can push aside, forms a good windbreaker.

Above: The Silky Terrier is a toy dog with a minimum of requirements. For all his energy and enthusiasm, he can do nicely with at least one outing and feeding daily. **Facing page:** The Alaskan Malamute is a large, hardy breed and one whose food and exercise requirements far exceed those of a toy breed.

Feeding Your Puppy

Dogs do not have the intelligence and self-control that cats exhibit when they delicately explore anything unexpected in the way of food. Hungry or not, most dogs will wolf down whatever is offered them and look for more. Puppies have even less sense, and yet most of them grow up in good health—even when their early diet has included wood splinters, old leather, and chance crickets or beetles. Nothing gives greater returns in health and vigor, good temper and long life, than a well-balanced diet, properly adapted to your particular dog's likes and needs.

When a pup takes to violent chewing of hard objects, he may be teething. This happens between the fourth and seventh months, and generally he manages pretty well by himself. If he should decide to cut his second teeth on your furniture or footgear, give him a happier alternative. When a puppy is teething, chewing something hard is helpful, but even then his sharp little teeth may crack a meat bone, and swallowed splinters may become lodged in his throat or intestines. Never should he have chicken, turkey or chop bones. Instead, train him to chew on Nylabone®, a pooch pacifier made of flavor-impregnated nylon that is recommended for countless hours of safe chewing. Unlike ordinary bones on the market, Nylabone becomes frizzled and frayed by the dog's chewing action and it massages the gums and teeth in the process. It will not splinter, despite the roughest treatment, and is safe for dogs of any size or age.

At the turn of the century, a major cause of death among dogs was malnutrition brought about by the inability to chew, which in turn was due to premature toothlessness. The dogs did not have the right elements in their food to develop bone, and they actually broke or lost teeth by gnawing so much on bones given them. Barring accidents, today's pet dog should live twice as long as a dog of 100 years ago and much longer than his own grandfather. Better feeding is 90 percent of the reason why.

So much for what he doesn't need. A book could be written on what he does need; yet it can be summed up briefly. The growth and development of your puppy depend upon proper feeding. A dog is a carnivorous animal, that is, he needs meat. To have only meat, however, would be as bad

Facing page: A litter of Yorkshire Terrier pups. Even though they are small dogs, "Yorkies" are more than happy to engage in the roisterous activities of the larger terrier breeds.

Facing page, top: Cocker Spaniel pups, like littermates of any breed, are affectionate towards one another. *Facing page, bottom:* As is typical of a puppy, this Shetland Sheepdog, or "Sheltie," is quite curious about this snoozing Old English Sheepdog. *Above:* A trio of Shelties owned by Ellen S. Gabriel.

as to have none. Milk, fish, eggs, cottage cheese, green vegetables and fruit are all good for him. Supplementary minerals, especially calcium, and vitamins help to support even the best diet.

Meat may be raw or cooked, since dogs can digest either. Too much starch is bad, but dogs assimilate starch contained in many well-cooked, thoroughly tested prepared kibbles and biscuits. Fat should always be included in the diet, especially in cold weather. A young, active dog needs more fat than a sluggish fireside pet. Your puppy will have been weaned before you get him, and the breeder probably will have started him on a five-meal-a-day routine, with meals of milk or equal parts evaporated milk and water; pre-cooked baby cereal or puppy meal in a thick, soupy consistency; a little cottage cheese; milk with a cooked egg;

The ears of German Shepherd Dog puppies, during the first few weeks or even the first few months of life, are down. As the dog matures and the muscles strengthen, they erect themselves.

Since 1952, *Tropical Fish Hobbyist* has been the source of accurate, up-to-the-minute, and fascinating information on every facet of the aquarium hobby. Join the more than 50,000 devoted readers world-wide who wouldn't miss a single issue.

Subscribe right now so you don't miss a single copy!

Adult Golden Retriever and its pups. Members of this breed are friendly, reliable, and trustworthy.

and, at first, scraped and then thoroughly ground beef. This is soon mixed with meal to form his first really solid diet.

You can probably begin on a four-a-day basis, feeding a milk combination mornings and the meat and meal mixture the last thing at night. Meal or kibble (broken chunks of hard dog biscuit) must be moistened by soaking in hot water. It absorbs about its own weight and is then mixed in equal amounts with the meat. You can soon go to three meals, spaced out and in increasing quantities. At about six months of age, two a day will be enough, and at a year, one. Always, of course, for good behavior or if he is very hungry, he can have a dog biscuit or "canine candy."

Amounts depend so much on the type of dog and his rate of growth that they are difficult to set. Check with a veterinarian if ever you're in doubt about how much and how often to feed your canine friend. A puppy should whirl in and

The Saint Bernard, a member of the Working Dog Group, is a strong, powerful dog.

clean up his dish but should never be allowed to stuff himself until his stomach is bloated and his sides hard. If he leaves food, it is a good sign he is being overfed. Cut back a bit on his rations, and, thereafter, be careful not to overdo it with his portions! If you have his interests really at heart, you will never give him quite all he can hold.

Besides meat, use other good foods containing protein. A bowl of cottage cheese may replace the baby-cereal mixture, or a cooked egg may be added to his morning milk, as a special treat. But meat and one of the good commercial meals should be the mainstays of his diet.

Table scraps? Add them, but a dog eating only scraps will lack stamina and resistance to disease. Dogs should never have potatoes; and give rice sparingly, although it is good in cases of bowel trouble. Any green or yellow vegetable may be added to the meat and meal mixture, particularly fine-cut carrots, asparagus ends, stringbeans—no other beans. You will note that as your dog gets older, he will often eat grass. This is a natural, sound instinct for cleansing his digestive system. Finely chopped lettuce or spinach will have the same effect when worked into the meat-meal

A Beagle puppy wearing the gentle and pleading expression that is characteristic of members of its breed.

mixture. Many dogs like tomatoes, cooked or raw.

Don't believe the superstition that milk makes worms or that raw meat gives a puppy fits. Onions or garlic add flavor, but do not prevent or kill worms. Don't let anyone tell you your dog should not have fat; without it, skin becomes scurfy and digestion is impeded. Cut up suet, add a good vegetable oil, or melt fat from beef or lamb and pour over the meal in cold weather.

Above all, puppies need calcium, the bone-maker. A spoonful of cod-liver oil or two or three drops of a vitamin preparation with two teaspoonsful of diphosphate of calcium sprinkled over the meal daily is the choice of many breeders. Others use commercial wafers or preparations combining these elements, which must be used together if the calcium is to be assimilated in the dog's system.

Once you hit a combination of foods that agrees with your dog and which he likes, stick to it. Dogs do not "get tired" of a regular diet; in fact, when a change must be made for some reason, it usually has to be gradual to keep the dog eating normally.

Never have food very hot or very cold. Warm up refrigerated meat, let kibble or meal stand until the water is well absorbed, and have the mixture lukewarm. Take up any food left after the puppy

has had 10 or 15 minutes to eat it. It is best to throw away what is left, but if it is absolutely fresh, the remainder may go into the refrigerator for the next feeding.

Keep food dishes and water pans clean. Renew water frequently, and keep it accessible always. After a heavy meal or hard romp, let the pup drink sparingly, however. If he vomits easily, a little bicarbonate of soda in the drinking water should help control the tendency.

With the proper nutrients in his diet, your puppy should develop healthy skin and coat. If, however, a certain amount of fatty acids are missing from his daily diet, he will lack the natural resilience that would allow him to withstand any severe or suddenly-changing climates. A well-balanced diet can provide the dog with the ability to withstand cold and hot climates. This is especially true in the winter, when an improper diet will cause the skin to become dry, a condition that will be accentuated by the cold, dry air of the season.

Facing page: A pair of Afghan Hound puppies looking quite a bit different than they will look when they are fully grown.

Extremes of cold seem easier for the dog to endure than those of heat. Eskimo dogs will cozily roll up in snowdrifts, their bushy tails protecting eyes and noses. Even shorthaired dogs will sit placidly in snow. What is worse than cold is chill. Always dry your dog's paws after they get wet, and rub the pup well after a romp in snow. (Half-dry isn't even half-safe, especially with a puppy!) For delicate breeds or dogs much exposed to steam heat, a water-shedding coat is a protection—it also makes mopping up easier. Believe it or not, it is not necessary to coddle your dog in winter.

A watchful Akita pup. Akitas are known for their alert and responsive temperament.

A blue merle Sheltie puppy. The term merle *is used to describe a coat coloration that is usually blue-gray with flecks of black.*

All breeds feel heat, though in varying degrees. Those with heavy coats should never be shaved. Normally, they shed to adapt to weather. The coat really serves as insulation against heat, for a dog can suffer severe sunburn on exposed skin. In bad heat, keep any dog quiet and discourage wild romps in the sun! Have fresh water always available, let him sleep all he wants during the day in a cool, dry cellar, under the porch or in long grass. Feed any heavy meal after dark.

When a puppy is really suffering from the heat, sponge him with cool water and give him ice to lick. This is one time you needn't be afraid to let him dry off naturally—it lowers body temperature.

Training Your Puppy

Be reassured! The process of teaching good manners isn't too difficult, and habits once formed are never forgotten.

If a puppy makes a puddle or otherwise sins, he has no sense of guilt until you show him you consider it wrong. He will not soil his bed if he can help it, but remember his retention capacity is small and his excreting organs must be emptied very often.

Put him outdoors at regular, frequent intervals. Dogs form habits quickly, and he will soon get the idea, especially if you praise and pat him generously when he has performed. At first, intervals of two hours are advisable. Time may be extended as he grows older. In severe weather, he may be broken to papers by taking him to a pile and placing him there patiently and often. Again, results should bring warm praise! The scent of a previously soiled paper on top will give him "ideas." Rush him out or to his papers if you see that certain look in this eye. If there is an accident, scold him, "No-no! Bad dog!" Never beat him for a mistake or frighten him by shouting roughly at him, and never rub his nose in his excreta.

The main thing about housebreaking is to give the little fellow frequent and regular chances to relieve himself, always immediately after he has eaten or when he has just woken up. Convey to him the idea that action

at certain times and places is good, and at others, very naughty. More than anything in the world, he wants to please you. Count on that. The dog's liking for routine is also in your favor. A dog is actually happier when the same thing happens at the same time every day. In any sort of training, work with that trait. Finally, remember that every dog must go out the last thing before going to bed. Make that excursion a fun one. Walk with your dog, talk to him; don't whisk him indoors the moment his duty is done. You both will sleep better for this pleasant, relaxing end of the day.

Now let's speak of the use of your voice in controlling your dog, for you may not realize how much its tone has to do with his behavior. Some dog owners seem to feel that the louder they yell, the better the dog will understand. On the contrary, a loud, harsh voice startles and frightens a sensitive puppy. Tone is everything in securing obedience.

Facing page: Patience and consistency are key elements of a successful puppy training program. Pictured is a Bichon Frise pup owned by Judith L. Hilmer.

For health reasons, your puppy's dining area should be separate from the area you have selected for paper training.

Many dog owners make the mistake of giving commands in long sentences that only another human being would understand. You get certain inflections in the dog's bark or whine, but only another dog understands "dog talk." Why should you expect your dog to understand all the words you use? True, your pet will love to hear you talk. Still, it is your tone that reaches and pleases him.

In his lifetime a dog comes to recognize many words, but he can be a well-trained, obedient pet by knowing just a few. He must know: "Come!," "Out?," "Stop it!," "No!," and "Down!" To them, add "Walk?," or "Want to go for a walk?," "Get in your chair!," "Go to bed!," or some such command to direct action, usually taught with

a gesture or by actually lifting the dog to the indicated spot. Of course, he soon knows "Good dog!" or "Bad boy." If you think though that he "understands every word," try bawling him out some time in a honey-sweet tone. That little tail will wag madly; it sounds mighty nice to him!

The most important word is his name. You may decide what you will call your puppy before you get him, or his name may come out of the blue, but do not delay choosing it. Use it every time you speak to him, over and over again, until he knows it as well as you do. Once he knows it, he will rush to respond because of your affectionate tone, or hang his head, ashamed, because your voice carries reproach.

He will soon learn your name, too, and those of other members of the family. To these, he will add the names of friends, neighboring children, and their dogs—names which will be useful in his daily life as your friendly, well-mannered pet.

The capacity to learn is born in every puppy, to a greater or lesser degree. Your puppy starts learning the moment he enters your house. (He starts learning about you and soon knows whether you or he will be the boss.) His capacity to learn grows as he does and is fully developed at the age of about a year. Although he eventually stops growing, he never stops learning. One way to train the puppy, and prepare him for more formal training when he is an adult, is to play with him. This may sound

Snuggling up with each other can help to strengthen the sense of security and well-being of these Beagle puppies.

simple, but in our busy lives we often fail to play with a new puppy as much as we should. At first he is a novelty, but it becomes "too much trouble" to give the time to him, and we tell the eager, bouncing little fellow to "be a good dog and lie down." He'd much rather be a good playfellow and later lie gladly at your feet for a snooze.

The game of fetch-and-carry, for instance. . .running after a ball or a stick, catching it and then bringing it back. . .is a chance for obedience training. The command "Go fetch!" may later be useful. Vary the game by substituting other items for the ball or stick. At first all these toys should be hidden in some place that is easy to find; then make it harder. Identify objects by word until he associates the word with the object—your slippers, the newspaper, etc. *Fetch* soon becomes a known word, and so does *find*, when you use them often for the same purpose.

A litter of Lhasa Apsos. Note the color variations possible within the breed.

Next comes the second command, "Bring it here." Some dogs are natural retrievers; others demand much patient practice as they want to run off with the ball, bury it, bite and pull at it, or even drop it and stroll off aimlessly. Keep at it until the puppy brings the object to you, winning high praise when he does. The third command is perhaps the hardest, again depending on the dog— "Drop it," or "Give it here."

The puppy who learns the rules of fetch-and-carry has taken a big step forward into being a well-trained adult dog. In this way, he also finds that learning can be fun.

Roughhousing (not *too* roughly) teaches him to play and not bite and to work to get something he wants, still without hurting the person holding it. In the course of a good rough and tumble, you will use words he will remember next time. He certainly will learn "Stop that," if he gets rough himself. If he needs reprimanding, a firm "No!" and a quick tap on the rump should make him behave.

You will find the little fellow actually inventing his own games. Absurd little routines may develop. When you return from a day at the office or a shopping trip, the pup may prod you to look for some hidden object, while he trots happily along on the search. If you both put on a terrific act when the lost item is found, you may be

Teach children to offer praise and an affectionate pat whenever the canine member of the household obeys a command.

greeted with this game every night!

Protect your puppy against what is really teasing, as when children call it "play" to steal his toys and hold them out of reach or to wrestle too roughly and hurt the little fellow. Never play with him, or let children do so, until the point of exhaustion. Be fair with him.

Reward him when you are teaching him something new, and let the play increase his understanding of you and your understanding of him. The time you spend with him can develop into a close bond that may someday stand you in good stead. He is learning, among other things, that you are *his owner.*

ADVANCED TRAINING

Training a dog does not mean harshly disciplining him. If you go about it properly, he will think it more fun than any game.

Some dogs are more obedient than others; few fail to recognize

Allowing your pet on furniture, as this Dachshund has been allowed, is a matter of personal choice.

the "I mean it" voice. Remain calm, firm, and repeat the words if necessary, time after time until obedience is given. Give praise, too, even if at first the pup hasn't quite made the grade, awarding at least an E for Effort.

Work with a puppy alone and not too long. His capacity to concentrate is limited, so give up when you see he has had all he can take. Try to stop on some achievement, which means praise, petting, perhaps a toothsome tidbit. If each session ends on a positive note, he'll welcome the next lesson.

Keep him on a long leash when teaching new lessons. He cannot run off or get away with ignoring your commands. Although you should work with him without other people or dogs around in the initial sessions, as he learns you can gradually train him to obey commands as they would be given in normal surroundings. He must obey not just when you are alone with him, but in all circumstances of ordinary daily life. Learning to behave in all situations is essential.

When he is older, he will enjoy (and so will you) attending the obedience classes held in every well-populated community. For most pets, however, home training is sufficient. This is particularly so for the fundamental obedience of the commands—"Come," "Sit" or "Down," the latter combined with "Stay!"

Some puppies seem to take naturally to the collar and leash; others have to be patiently accustomed to the restraint and guidance that they provide. Start yours with a narrow collar, giving as little contact around the neck as possible. Be sure it is loose enough for comfort but not so loose that he can back out of it, or scratch it over his head. An appeal to vanity may help here. Make a great fuss about how *beautiful* he

looks in his new adornment. Repeat the word *collar* always in a tone of excitement and pleasure. The same tone helps "sell" the word *leash*.

Some pet owners never put a collar on a pup when he is indoors. However, it has the advantage—if put on immediately in the morning and taken off at bedtime—of suggesting to the puppy that he is dressed for the day. Sometimes a pup will bring the collar to his owner's bedside to suggest that it is time to get going. Also, the collar that is on all the time is a convenience to the owner—it's easier to grab and catch a collar, as a puppy dashes by, than soft, slippery skin! A word of warning: if your pup is turned loose in a fenced yard, be sure the collar will not catch on a post or protruding wire. Unfortunate puppies, and grown dogs too, have hung themselves this way.

Now for the leash. It is usually advised that you attach it to the collar and let the puppy run indoors, or in the yard, with it trailing. I feel that this may scare him more than it helps to get him accustomed. After all, what he must learn is that he is at one end, a human being at the other. Pulling after him, it may catch under a chair leg or a tree stump and frighten him by the sudden jerk. From the beginning, it is the angle at which it is held—showing the connection between pet and owner—and the association of

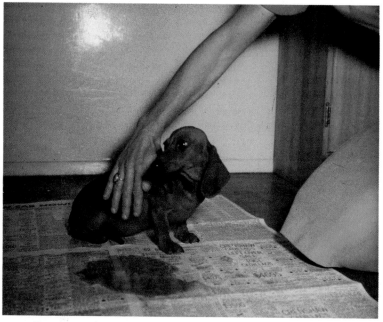

Be generous in your praise when your puppy uses the paper properly.

pleasure that must be learned. "Leash practice" can and should be fun. If the puppy is timid, walk him up and down indoors, pulling gently and coaxing to keep him in motion and in line with your own progress. Then try it in the yard, on the lawn, or up and down a quiet street. Never jerk violently, or choke him if he sits and refuses

to move, and don't insist on absolute accuracy in following your footsteps. Let the little fellow wander off at will; if he sits down, pat and laugh at him a bit, and wait a moment or two before beginning to get him going. He will soon realize that the leash is a tie between him and you.

Incidentally, dogs learn more

quickly from other dogs than from human beings. If you have a friend with an older, leash-trained dog, walking together will soon put the idea over to your puppy. When he finds that the leash means "We're going out!" it becomes a friend, not a foe. Like the collar, it is a signal he soon learns—and will bring to *your* attention when he wants action! You are teaching him this when you pick it up and say "Here's your LEASH—we're going for a WALK!"

At first, start with your pup on a long leash. Go as far away from him as the leash permits, then call "Come (dog's name)!" As you do this, give the leash a little jerk toward you. If he resists, pull gently, and the moment he is within reaching distance, pet and praise him. Next time, he will resist less and will soon come on your command.

If you want to have him run

A choke chain can be helpful regardless of the size of breed you are training. Properly used, it controls the dog with a minimum of discomfort.

loose and come on whistle, practice that first with the long leash. If you have an enclosed yard, you can discard the leash or rope as soon as he seems to be getting the idea, and practice with the call or whistle. If he is interested in something else and slow to answer, keep repeating in a crisp, firm—not cross—voice until he obeys. If he comes to you more or less by accident, pet and praise! It's all right to use dog candy or another tidbit as a reward, but not so regularly that he will expect it. Petting and praise are always the best rewards and always should be given. Remember, when he does

come, don't let the little fellow jump on you. That's a bad habit he can easily form. Bend over, holding him down, while you pat him and if he tries to jump, keep interjecting the word *down* with the *good boy* and his name.

The "Sit" is taught on a short leash, holding the puppy closely beside you. The command is accompanied by a firm push on his hindquarters, and again, praise when the result is achieved. Most trainers hold the leash in the left hand, use the right to push the dog down and pat him when successful. It doesn't matter in the least if you are left-handed and do it the other way. It is best to

When several puppies are being fed together, always make sure that they all get an equal share of food.

The Cocker Spaniel is quite popular as a family pet and companion.

alternate so that he doesn't get the idea that he is to sit *only* in a certain spot or attitude. You want the association to be with the

word, so that he will sit at any time, on command.

In the same way, teach "Down," starting with the puppy as he now obeys "Sit," then pulling his front legs gently forward as you say the word *down.* If you use *down* whenever he shows a tendency to jump, you may want to teach this as a two-word command: "Lie down."

"Stay" needs considerable practice. You can teach him to *stay* either seated or lying down. By repeated practice, say "Stay," walking away, and acting shocked if he rises and follows. Take him back and go through it again. Always, of course, return to praise him mightily when he has "stayed" for even a few brief seconds. Gradually lengthen the time. You can perfect this obedience

Above: *A family of handsome Labrador Retrievers.* **Facing page:** *Even as a pup, the Bichon Frise quickly develops a heavy coat.*

command while moving about at housework or in a cellar workshop; it needn't take too much time after the idea has been implanted.

Your dog should also learn to walk on a leash without pulling; the command "Heel" is often used here. As with "Stay," practice makes perfect. He should also be taught some signal to use when he wants to go out. The appropriate bark for *speak* means he will let you know, if you do not see him at the door, that he needs to go out. He should learn not to jump on people, and having him "Sit" as a new friend approaches will control his enthusiasm. He also should not bark and dash forward at anyone, even a suspected interloper, until given a command. He should not be allowed on furniture, unless you permit him on one special chair; he also should not beg for food at the table, although here it is often the family that must be trained, not the dog!

You should see that he is not allowed to wander the neighborhood, making a nuisance of himself. and that he never runs loose in the street. The dog should not go off your premises without being on a leash.

Everything you teach him to do or not to do will help at some time. If the leash breaks or he gets outdoors without a collar, obeying your call *may save his life.*

An owner of obedience-trained spaniels once failed to close her house door when she went to cross the street to her car. Looking back, she saw to her horror two eager little fellows loping down the front steps—and an automobile coming down the street. She called "Down!" raising her arm in the obedience-taught gesture. Instantly, the little things dropped flat, and the car whizzed past between them and their mistress. Not till she called "Come!" did they rise and trot happily to her.

Obedience training won't "make a robot" of your dog. It certainly will make a better citizen of him— and who knows?—of you. That's all we could ask, isn't it?

Facing page: Bloodhounds are renowned for their ability to trail a scent. These puppies exhibit the docile, shy demeanor that is characteristic of members of the breed.

Caring For Your Puppy

When we talk of dogs' ailments, the subject of worms comes up first. Many dog owners worm their own pets with standard commercial preparations. However, a veterinarian's diagnosis should come first, and it is wise to have him do the job.

There are several kinds of worms, and no one medicine will reach them all. Except for roundworms, which may be seen at times, and tapeworms, in which flat, white segments appear, these pests must be identified by microscopic examination of the stool. A veterinarian may discover more types than one. It saves mess and bother, as well as giving your pet professional care in dosage of medicines that can be poisonous, to have worming done by an expert.

Symptoms of severe worm infestation are pot-bellies or excessive thinness; a hacking, recurrent cough (with roundworms sometimes being vomited); loose bowels with slimy matter; and, on occasion, even convulsions. If you see your pup rub or drag his rear end along the floor, have him tested for worms at once. Hookworms, which are a serious problem, give a pale, bloodless look to the normally pink mouth, and the eyes may be sunken and dull. There may be blood in the stools, vomiting, and rapid loss of weight. These and the tiny, ugly whipworms are nothing for the amateur to fool with. Incidentally, if a puppy drags himself along the floor, without showing other symptoms of worm infestation, it may be that the oil glands alongside the anus need emptying. Sometimes they get clogged, and a veterinarian can quickly press the matter out. He will show you how to do it if this occurs.

The scratching dog is a nuisance to himself and others. It may be that he scratches because of fleas. Fleabites make the skin so sensitive that long after the pests are routed, the itching may go on. Use a soothing lotion or powder to lessen the irritation. While the itching may be from summer eczema, in any season be sure the skin is not overly dry as a result of too little fat in the diet.

Scratching may be from vitamin deficiency, but may go into eczema as a result of the raking nails. Here, diet is of prime importance. All these are things about which your veterinarian can advise you, though usually simple

Facing page: Watching your child build a trusting relationship with pets, such as between this youngster and her Shar-Pei puppies, can be one of the many joys of owning a pet.

home remedies preceded, accompanied, and followed by good diet and *complete cleanliness* will control the situation.

To discuss diseases that may attack dogs would require an entire book. Suffice it to say that all-around care, like feeding, is the preventive of trouble. The person from whom you buy your puppy, or your veterinarian, will inform you how to give simple medicine if necessary.

Two types of inoculations are as necessary for the peace of mind of the owner as for the

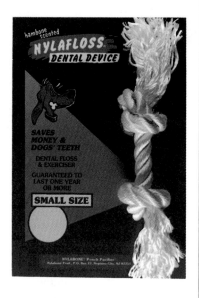

health of the puppy. Many communities make it compulsory to have anti-rabies shots given once a year. If your puppy is under six months of age, your veterinarian may prefer to give him a "booster" shot, until he is old enough for the regular dosage.

By all means, know your veterinarian and have him know your dog. As with a baby, a dog cannot tell you "where it hurts," and to take one to a doctor for the first time when it is sick or in pain is not fair to patient or veterinarian. "Introduce" the puppy at some casual visit, with the veterinarian going over him for general condition, or for possible worming. Choose a veterinarian who knows small animals and is interested in the type of dog you have.

Other dog owners will advise you, and there are good books on care and feeding; but to fail to take your dog to a veterinarian in time won't necessarily save bills—it may double them.

Distemper is the great killer, particularly of young puppies. Don't fail to have your pup given the series of shots which

Nylafloss® Dental Device, available at your local pet shop is designed to function much like human dental floss. The durable nylon strands help dislodge plaque and tartar between the teeth and beneath the gum line where periodontal problems begin.

An inquisitive Rottweiler pup owned by Kathy Thompson of Von Gailingen Rottweilers.

immunize him against this extremely contagious and often fatal disease. Usually, two serum shots are given, followed by one of virus, which actually starts a mild form of the disease but gives immunity thereafter.

A disease that can spread with lightning rapidity is infectious hepatitis. It attacks the liver and is almost always fatal. It is possible for your dog to have a shot for this, combined with the ones for distemper. If hepatitis has been known in your community, by all

means have your puppy or grown dog inoculated.

The dog's medicine chest should contain a thermometer to take temperatures rectally, milk of magnesia or mineral oil for mild constipation, and a remedy for diarrhea. Also recommended are petroleum jelly for a rough nose, bicarbonate of soda to clean his teeth, a disinfectant, a good flea powder, clean combs and brushes, a "dry bath" preparation, and a nail clipper. Borrow simple

A litter of Bichon Frise puppies. Owner, Judith L. Hilmer.

emergency remedies for cuts, burns, heat strokes, etc. (iodine, Epsom salts, aromatic spirits of ammonia, castor oil) from your own medicine chest as needed.

Opinions differ on how often to bathe a dog. There are times when nothing but a tub bath with

CARING FOR YOUR PUPPY

soap and hard scrubbing will clean a dirty puppy or grown dog. Be sure to use a safe soap, apply lavishly in thick lather, rub in, rinse, repeat and rinse thoroughly. Have the water warm, and thoroughly get all the soap out. Keep it out of the eyes, of course, and wash the visible parts of the ears gently with a little cotton on a fingertip. Then get your dog dry!

An occasional treat is fine, but don't teach your pet to expect a food reward every time he obeys a command.

Never let him go out or wander around a chilly house half-dry.

There is one time when a bath is essential—when a female is over her season. This semi-annual experience is not difficult to manage if you approach it sensibly; watchfulness is the keynote.

Someone has said, "A female comes in season every six months; a male is always in." If you have chosen a female for your pet, you should watch her from the time she is about six months old, as she may "come in" any time thereafter. You will see a swelling of the vulva and a discharge, straw-colored at first, gradually turning red.

She should be confined—indoors, in a kitchen or dry cellar, with plenty of newspapers, or outdoors in a well-enclosed yard. You can safely walk her on leash by spraying her with a commercial preparation which repels the males. Be especially careful as her flow lessens; she becomes willing to accept the male as the swelling subsides. After about 21 days, swelling will have disappeared, as will the discharge, and she loses interest in other dogs. When she has finished her heat cycle, give her a thorough bath with a good dog soap and restore her to polite society.

The word *grooming* applies largely to coat, but it also goes further and is definitely allied to health. Brushing not only cleans skin, but it tones up circulation and growth of hair. On small or wiry-haired dogs, use a brush with fairly soft bristles or a grooming

When clipping your pup's nails, hold the paw firmly in one hand, and clip carefully with the other hand.

The security of a soft toy animal is all this Golden Retriever pup needs to be content in dreamland.

glove. A longhaired dog is better groomed by a brush with larger, stiffer bristles, or one of the metal combs that have teeth well set apart. Never comb a dog's hair with such a sharp comb that you scratch the skin. It may start itching and scratching—in any case, he'll hate grooming if it hurts in any way.

Also, if your dog is very wet, don't comb his coat while matted, and never at any time tear at snarls or burrs. All mats should be removed prior to the bath, as this only tightens the snarl. Coax the hairs out of tangles gently with the fingers and a small, smooth comb, and if the tangle is bad and your puppy frightened, just cut it out.

Hair does grow again, and quickly, you know! A word to the wise: keep your beloved dog from getting tangled or matted by brushing him often.

A word for you as well as the puppy—a well-brushed dog sheds less on furniture, scratches less because of skin irritation, and gets used to being handled and groomed so that when you do have to bathe him he will be unafraid and easier to rub and dry off afterwards.

Once bathed, you can keep any dog clean without tubbing for a long time. Many dogs, with beautiful glossy coats and no "doggy odor," are bathed perhaps twice a year. The secret is brushing regularly—every day. Have a set time for it. Your puppy will enjoy it. He likes to be clean, likes the friction of the stiff brush, likes being with you and your voice as you talk and admire him, for let no one tell you that dogs haven't any vanity!

Care of the paws is imperative—inspect them regularly. Look for cuts (which should be bathed and dabbed with iodine), ticks, possible stones or sticks caught between the toes or under the pad, and toenail problems. Too-long nails may catch and pull out, hurting the paw and making it raw so that infection may set in. If much too long, they throw the foot back on the ankle—"down on the pasterns" is the correct term. Running on gravel or small stones abrades the nails, as does steady and regular walking on concrete or asphalt. But even so, nails have to be cut occasionally.

To cut a tiny puppy's toenails, sharp small scissors are strong enough, but as the nail thickens and toughens, clippers are better. With either, cut the nail straight across, filing a rough edge if necessary. Unless your pup is hurt or frightened, the process will be simple. The secret is to hold the paw firmly, cut quickly and surely, but not too deep. It is better to cut nails soon again than cut too close to the quick, perhaps drawing blood and frightening the puppy and yourself.

Facing page: If introduced when they are young, puppies of different breeds can be great pals. Pictured are a Bassett Hound pup and a Dachshund pup.

An adult German Shepherd Dog and its pup. **Below:** The pup and kitten that are raised together will gladly share a household.

Environment
and
Exercise

Your new puppy will need some time to become adjusted to his new environment, as he finds that he is no longer surrounded by his loving and attentive mother and littermates. Thus, the socialization that the pup will now have to undergo relies entirely upon you. Whether he is to become a well-behaved dog enjoyed by the neighbors or a barking menace will depend on the training and amount and quality of attention you show him.

The ease with which a new pup will adjust to your home life will amaze you, and before very long you'll be boring your friends by bragging that: "He understands every word we say. He can do everything but talk." It will be true, too.

If you don't make a prior commitment that your dog is an important member of your family, the dog will not fit into his environment. He'll come up with unsuspected character faults, and instead of bragging about him, you'll be asking the experts how to break him of this and that habit.

We've all heard it said that a human's brain and character are capable of developing to limitless heights and that no human minds have ever been developed to their full capacity. This is also true of dogs. In the case of the dog, environment is a major factor in determining character development.

You can't tie your dog out in the backyard day and night and expect him to be anything but stupid and frustrated. Nor can you tie him downstairs in the basement. He would quite literally go crazy. He will understand that he's not wanted in the home, and he'll come to regard himself as a prisoner. The result can only be severe frustration and trouble for everyone.

If you have strong feelings about having certain areas of the house "off limits" to your dog, you can teach him that he can't come into, say, the bedrooms. However, make sure he understands that he is permitted to come into the living room and kitchen, and possibly other frequently used rooms. Most importantly, he should be allowed to take part in family gatherings whenever such are held. He then knows that he really belongs, and the rewards in terms of the loyalty and affection that he gives you will be proportionate.

Generally, the larger the dog the more exercise he will require. This is especially true during the time that the dog is actively growing. Most people mistakenly believe that dogs, as well as humans, need less and less exercise as they mature. It must be remembered that muscles left relatively "unused" for long periods will eventually weaken. Thus, regular exercise is a necessity for maintaining proper muscle tone and increasing the capabilities of the cardiovascular system. Just as a doctor will tell you the best exercise for you, your dog's veterinarian is the best one to offer advice on a daily exercise regime for your dog. Of course, while your dog is still a pup he will undoubtedly get more than enough exercise in exploring his surroundings.

A puppy exercises himself in many ways, one of them being the practice of chasing his tail. That's a game that dogs, along with the wild foxes and wolves, have invented for themselves. Puppies will quickly recognize games that you invent for them and enthusiastically join in, fetching things, rolling over and performing similar stunts. These are sometimes called tricks, but they are fine forms of exercise as well.

Studies of dogs have shown that dogs aren't especially happy when turned loose to rove. Yet, if abandoned in this way, they adapt themselves to this situation and become incurable rovers. They run away at every opportunity. They come home only to eat, rest and sleep. Roving becomes the only environment they know and can believe in.

On the other hand, dogs kept primarily in the house go almost crazy with joy when taken for escorted walks by their owners. This can be on or off the leash— *on* it on busy streets, *off* it when inviting vacant lots or fields are reached. Of course, it cannot be overemphasized how important it is to keep the leash *on* your dog unless you are in a secluded area totally free of traffic hazards.

Such walks will give the dog the exercise he needs, but more importantly, they give him companionship and a sense of belonging. Many an owner brags that his dog brings his own leash or sits patiently by the door anticipating the daily walk. Actions such as these are proof positive of the enjoyment a dog gets from these outings.

Allow your puppy sufficient time to rest after he has played or been exercised.

Many people feel that it is undesirable to take dogs for walks along city streets, citing that the dogs may relieve themselves on other people's lawns, scratch up flowers or wet on plants along the walk. Some enthusiastic walkers develop an uncontrollable desire to "see the world." This could translate itself into running away when, because you must be away or are sick, the daily pattern of your walks has to be interrupted.

Facing page: A lovable mixed breed pup resting comfortably with his feline friend. *Above:* This cat doesn't seem too pleased by this puppy's friendly overtures! *Right:* The adult Saint Bernard, although very large in size, is just as gentle as he is when a pup.

You can accustom your dog to staying in your own yard by taking him out to play in it. Don't put him out and think he'll amuse himself. Take him out and play with him. He'll get his exercise, and come to feel that the only place in the world he can rightfully play is in his own backyard.

If you start this sort of exercise when you first get your puppy, he'll be a little afraid of the big wide world outside the yard. Give him a few scoldings if he tends to go beyond the borders of the yard during play, as this will fix in his mind forever that his environment—his world—is within the confines of your home and backyard.

When you have that kind of dog, he'll be a joy to own. Moreover, he'll be the pride, not the pest, of the entire neighborhood.

Charm and innocence are personified in this pair of Labrador Retriever puppies.

Left and Above: Longhaired breeds need regular grooming to keep their coats looking their best. **Below:** Siberian Husky pups are attractive to a prospective buyer, as they are happily active dogs. **Facing page:** An affectionate pair of Westies.

Final Preparations

THE PUPPY'S FIRST NIGHT WITH YOU

The puppy's first night at home is likely to be disturbing to the family. Keep in mind that suddenly being away from his mother, brothers and sisters is a new experience for him; he may be confused and frightened. If you have a special room in which you have his bed, be sure that there is nothing there with which he can harm himself. Be sure that all lamp cords are out of his reach and that there is nothing that he can tip or pull over. Check furniture that he might get stuck under or behind and objects that he might chew. If you want him to sleep in your room, he probably will be quiet all night, reassured by your presence. If left in a room by himself he will cry and howl, and you will have to steel yourself to be impervious to his whining. After a few nights alone he should adjust. The first night that he is alone it is wise to put a loud-ticking alarm clock, as well as his toys, in the room with him. The alarm clock will make a comforting noise, and he will not feel that he is alone.

YOUR PUPPY'S BED

Every dog likes to have a place that is his alone. He holds nothing more sacred than his own bed, whether it be a rug, dog crate, or dog bed. If you get your puppy a bed, be sure to get one which discourages chewing. Also be sure that the bed is large enough to be comfortable for him when he is full grown. Locate it away from drafts and radiators. A word might be said here in defense of the crate, which many pet owners think is cruel and confining. Given a choice, a young dog instinctively selects a secure place in which to lounge, rest or sleep. The walls and ceiling of a crate, even a wire one, answer that need. Once he regards his crate as a safe and reassuring place to stay, you will be able to leave him alone in the house.

ALL DOGS NEED TO CHEW

Puppies and young dogs need something with resistance to chew on while their teeth and jaws are developing—for cutting the puppy teeth, to induce growth of the permanent teeth under the puppy teeth, to assist in getting rid of the puppy teeth at the proper time, to help the permanent teeth through the gums, to assure normal jaw development and to settle the permanent teeth solidly in the jaws.

Facing page: A Golden Retriever exhibiting his fondness for his Nylabone®, a therapeutic device designed to satisfy a dog's need to chew. (This dog is owned by Anthony J. Vitti.)

The Cocker Spaniel
can be a wonderful,
gentle-natured pet, as
is proved by this pup's
ability to get along with
his Persian companion.
The Cocker is well
suited to family life, as
it gets along fine with
children. Still, if the
Cocker is to live with
just one person, it will
become loyally devoted
to its master.

The adult dog's desire to chew stems from the instinct for tooth cleaning, gum massage and jaw exercise—plus the need for an outlet for periodic doggie tensions.

Dental caries as they affect the teeth of humans is virtually unknown in dogs—but tartar accumulates on the teeth of dogs, particularly at the gum line, more rapidly than on the teeth of

Puppies six weeks old can spend some time outdoors provided the weather is mild, and there is sun.

humans. These accumulations, if not removed, bring irritation, and then infection which erodes the tooth enamel and ultimately destroys the teeth at the roots.

Most chewing by adult dogs is an effort to do something about this problem for themselves.

Tooth and jaw development will normally continue until the dog is more than a year old—but sometimes much longer, depending upon the breed, chewing exercise, the rate at which calcium can be utilized and many other factors, known and unknown, which affect the development of individual dogs. Diseases, like distemper for example, may sometimes arrest development of the teeth and

This youngster is offering his Labrador Retriever a Gumadisc®, a flexible floppy flying disc that can provide hours of fun and exercise for both a dog and its owner. Always be sure to supervise young children when they are playing with their canine pals. (Pictured is Nicholas Bajada with Misty, owned by John Buhagiar.)

Above, left: *Saint Bernard with his Spitz pup pal.* **Above, right:** *The Scottish Terrier makes a fine pet.* **Left:** *This Yorkie pup is tiny enough to fit into this glass jar.* **Facing page:** *Snoozing peacefully are this Cocker Spaniel pup and his feline friend.*

jaws, which may resume months, or even years later.

This is why dogs, especially puppies and young dogs, will often destroy property worth hundreds of dollars, when their chewing instinct is not diverted from their owner's possessions, particularly during the widely varying critical period for young dogs.

Saving your possessions from destruction, assuring proper development of teeth and jaws, providing for "interim" tooth cleaning and gum massage, and channeling doggie tensions into a non-destructive outlet are, therefore, all dependent upon the dog having something suitable for chewing readily available when his instinct tells him to chew. If your purposes, and those of your dog, are to be accomplished, what you provide for chewing must be desirable from the doggie viewpoint, have the necessary functional qualities, and above all, be safe for your dog.

It is very important that dogs not be permitted to chew on anything they can break, or indigestible things from which they can bite sizeable chunks. Sharp pieces, from such as a bone which can be broken by a dog, may pierce the intestine wall and kill. Indigestible things which can be bitten off in chunks, such as toys made of rubber compound or cheap plastic, may cause an intestinal stoppage if not regurgitated—to bring painful death, unless surgery

is promptly performed.

Strong natural bones, such as 4- to 8- inch lengths of round shin bone from mature beef—either the kind you can get from your butcher or one of the variety available commercially in pet stores—may serve your dog's teething needs, if his mouth is large enough to handle them effectively.

You may be tempted to give your puppy a smaller bone, and he may not be able to break it when you do—but puppies grow rapidly, and the power of their jaws constantly increases until maturity. This means that a growing dog may break one of the smaller bones at any time, swallow the pieces and die before you realize what is wrong.

Many people make the mistake of thinking of their dog's teeth in terms of the teeth of the wild carnivores or those of the dog in antiquity. The teeth of wild carnivorous animals and the teeth found in the fossils of the dog-like creatures of antiquity have far thicker and stronger enamel than those of our contemporary dogs.

Facing page: This litter of German Shepherd Dog puppies gives their mother little time for rest!

*Right: The Irish Setter is a highly attractive breed whose function as a hunting dog tends to be overlooked by prospective buyers. Most people are so charmed by the breed's beauty that they fail to recognize the hunting potential. **Below and facing page, bottom:** In quiet slumber are two King Charles Spaniels.*

All hard natural bones are highly abrasive. If your dog is an avid chewer, natural bones may wear away his teeth prematurely; hence, they then should be taken away from your dog when the teething purposes have been served. The badly worn, and usually painful, teeth of many mature dogs can be traced to excessive chewing on natural bones.

Contrary to popular belief, knuckle bones which can be chewed up and swallowed by the dog provide little, if any, useable calcium or other nutriment. They do, however, disturb the digestion of most dogs and cause them to vomit the nourishing food they need.

An old leather shoe is another popular answer to the chewing need—but be very sure that the rubber heel, all nails, and other metal parts such as lace grommets, metal arches, etc., have been removed. Be especially careful to get all of the nails. A chunk of rubber heel can cause an intestinal stoppage. If it has a nail in it, the intestine wall may be pierced or torn. Then there is, of course, always the hazard that your dog may fail to differentiate between his shoe and yours, and eat up a good pair while you're not looking.

Dried rawhide products of various types, shapes, sizes and prices have come on the market during the past few years. They don't serve the primary chewing functions very well, they are a bit messy when wet from mouthing, and most dogs chew them up rather rapidly. A number of cases of death, and near death, by strangulation have been reported to be the result of partially

Left: Airedale pup owned by Victorianne Curtis. Facing page: Adult Pomeranian and its youngster. Owner, Jacqueline Rayner.

Left: This Sheltie may be enjoying a Christmas stocking, but your pet should actually be trained to stay away from such ornaments, which are potentially dangerous to him. **Below:** The Scottie is an intelligent, active breed of dog.

swallowed chunks of rawhide swelling in the throat. More recently, some veterinarians have been attributing cases of acute constipation to large pieces of incompletely digested rawhide in the intestine.

The nylon bones are probably the most complete, safe and economical answer to the chewing need. Dogs cannot break them or bite off sizeable chunks; hence, they are completely safe. Being longer lasting than other things offered for the purpose, they are economical.

Hard chewing raises little bristle-like projections on the surface of the nylon bones, providing effective interim tooth cleaning and vigorous gum massage, much in the same way your toothbrush does it for you. The little projections are raked off and swallowed in the form of thin shavings—but the chemistry of the nylon is such that they break down in the stomach fluids and pass through without effect.

The toughness of the nylon provides the strong chewing resistance needed for important jaw exercise and effective help for the teething functions—but there is no tooth wear because nylon is non-abrasive.

Nylabone® is highly recommended by veterinarians as a safe, healthy nylon bone that can't splinter or chip. Instead, Nylabone is frizzled by the dog's chewing action, creating a toothbrush-like surface that cleanses the teeth and massages the gums. Nylabone products are available in your local pet shop.

Nothing, however, substitutes for periodic professional attention to your dog's teeth and gums, not any more than your toothbrush can do that for you. Have your dog's teeth cleaned by your veterinarian at least once a year.

Index

Overleaf: These children are handling the new member of the family in the correct way: gently and with kindness.

PUPPIES
KW-023